Becoming a Woman Who

Loves

CYNTHIA HEALD

Love is patient, love is kind. It does not envy, it does
not boast, it is not proud. . . . Love never fails.

1 Corinthians 13:4, 8, NIV

NAVPRESS

A NavPress resource published in alliance
with Tyndale House Publishers, Inc.

NavPress is the publishing ministry of The Navigators, an international Christian organization and leader in personal spiritual development. NavPress is committed to helping people grow spiritually and enjoy lives of meaning and hope through personal and group resources that are biblically rooted, culturally relevant, and highly practical.

For more information, visit www.NavPress.com.

Becoming a Woman Who Loves

Copyright © 2009 by Cynthia Heald. All rights reserved.
This book was originally published by Thomas Nelson in 2002.

A NavPress resource published in alliance with Tyndale House Publishers, Inc.

Visit the author's website at www.cynthiaheald.com.

NAVPRESS and the NAVPRESS logo are registered trademarks of NavPress, The Navigators, Colorado Springs, CO. *TYNDALE* is a registered trademark of Tyndale House Publishers, Inc. Absence of ® in connection with marks of NavPress or other parties does not indicate an absence of registration of those marks.

The Team:
Don Pape, Publisher
Caitlyn Carlson, Acquisitions Editor
Jennifer Ghionzoli, Designer

Author photo by Shelly Han Photography, copyright © 2016. All rights reserved.

Cover vintage border copyright © Vintage Style Designs/Creative Market. All rights reserved.
Cover typeface and floral illustration copyright © Lisa Glanz/Creative Market. All rights reserved.
Cover font by Laura Worthington/Creative Market. All rights reserved.

Unless otherwise indicated, all Scripture quotations are taken from the *Holy Bible*, New Living Translation, copyright © 1996, 2004, 2015 by Tyndale House Foundation. Used by permission of Tyndale House Publishers, Inc., Carol Stream, Illinois 60188. All rights reserved. Scripture quotations marked MSG are taken from *THE MESSAGE* by Eugene H. Peterson, copyright © 1993, 1994, 1995, 1996, 2000, 2001, 2002. Used by permission of NavPress Publishing Group. All rights reserved. Scripture quotations marked NIV are taken from the Holy Bible, *New International Version*,® *NIV*.® Copyright © 1973, 1978, 1984, 2011 by Biblica, Inc.® Used by permission. All rights reserved worldwide. Scripture quotations marked NKJV are taken from the New King James Version,® copyright © 1982 by Thomas Nelson, Inc. Used by permission. All rights reserved. Scripture verses marked *Phillips* are taken from *The New Testament in Modern English* by J. B. Phillips, copyright © J. B. Phillips, 1958, 1959, 1960, 1972. All rights reserved. Scripture verses marked WMS are taken from the *Williams New Testament* by Charles B. Williams, © 1937, 1965, 1966, by Edith S. Williams, Moody Bible Institute of Chicago.

ISBN 978-1-61521-023-7

Printed in the United States of America

22	21	20	19	18	17	16
7	6	5	4	3	2	1

Watch what God does, and then you do it, like children who learn proper behavior from their parents. Mostly what God does is love you. Keep company with him and learn a life of love. Observe how Christ loved us. His love was not cautious but extravagant. He didn't love in order to get something from us but to give everything of himself to us. Love like that.

EPHESIANS 5:1-2, MSG

So, chosen by God for this new life of love, dress in the wardrobe God picked out for you: compassion, kindness, humility, quiet strength, discipline. Be even-tempered, content with second place, quick to forgive an offense. Forgive as quickly and completely as the Master forgave you. And regardless of what else you put on, wear love. It's your basic, all-purpose garment. Never be without it.

COLOSSIANS 3:12-14, MSG

Contents

Preface

WHILE READING IN THE GOSPEL of John, I was struck with the command that Jesus gave to His disciples on the night of His betrayal. He was sharing His last words with His band of men—important, significant words to be remembered and taken to heart: "A new commandment I give to you, that you love one another; as I have loved you, that you also love one another. By this all will know that you are My disciples, if you have love for one another" (John 13:34-35, NKJV).

As I read these words, I thought, *What is the old commandment? The old commandment is to love my neighbor as I love myself.* As I considered the old and new commands, I realized that I liked the old commandment better! The new commandment raised the standard for loving. *I think it is easier to love others as I love myself,* I thought. *How could I possibly love as Jesus loved? He loved sacrificially, unconditionally, and passionately. He forgave; He was patient; He didn't mind being interrupted.*

The two greatest commands are to love God and to love others, and I realize that this new commandment was given by Jesus to the disciples and therefore to the church. It is by our love for each other that the world can see that we are His disciples. So even though this command is special to the body of Christ, I was still challenged with the thought of studying the personal implications of this new commandment for my own life. Could I really learn to love as Jesus loved? What exactly would this love look like? Could I actually grow in this love so that it would become a part of my daily life? What would this godly love cost me?

With no little hesitancy, I began to study how to become a woman who loves. I knew it would not be easy; in fact, it has been incredibly convicting. But it has also been life changing. Any time love is pursued, the pursuer can never be the same, for it is the nature of love to transform.

As a result of this study, my understanding of love has broadened. Now I realize how critical godly love is to the body of Christ and to the world around us. I have been challenged to come before the Lord selflessly and willingly, allowing Him to teach me to grow continually in love. Christ desires that all His disciples love one another with His love. My prayer is that as you take time to study and pray over the Scriptures and questions we discuss, you will become a woman who loves the Lord and others wholeheartedly and passionately.

My benediction is the same as Paul's to the Thessalonians: "May the Lord make your love for one another and for all people grow and overflow, just as our love for you overflows. May he, as a result, make your hearts strong, blameless, and holy as you stand before God our Father" (1 Thessalonians 3:12-13).

Cynthia Heald

Suggestions

-FOR USING THIS STUDY-

THIS BIBLE STUDY HAS BEEN created to help you search the Scriptures and draw closer to God as you seek to grow in Christlike love. All you need is a Bible, a writing tool, and an expectant heart. You may find it helpful, however, to have access to supplemental resources such as a Bible translation in addition to the one you normally use, a general dictionary, a general Bible commentary, a Bible handbook, or a study Bible with reference notations.

Becoming a Woman Who Loves is appropriate for individual as well as group use, and for women of any age and season of life. Before you begin each chapter, pray for attentiveness to how God is speaking to you through His Word and for sensitivity to His prompting. At the conclusion of each chapter, you will have the opportunity to write out whatever God may be prompting you to learn, reflect on, or apply. Ask God to direct your response to this personalized question so that you might receive His abundant love for you, which will in turn supply the love you give to others.

Adding Scripture memorization to this practice will help you abide in the love of Christ, the True Vine, day by day. Write the memory verses (from your favorite version) on a card or Post-it, put it in a place where you will see it regularly, and memorize it. Thank God for who He is and for what He is doing in your life.

Quotations from Christian writers are included to help you understand the biblical content of each chapter and to enhance your personal response to God's Word.

The Bible has much to say about the importance of learning from and encouraging one another in the community of believers. If you are using this study with a small group, the questions and exercises that are provided will give you excellent opportunities for talking and praying together about loving one another as Christ loves you.

The Father spoke:

My child, do you know that I love you?

Yes, Father, I know that You love me.

How do you know of My love?

You sent Your Son to die on the cross for my sins. You have
adopted me as Your own child. You have given me Your
Holy Spirit, who has transformed my heart with Your love.

Since you have freely received My love, do you freely love others?

I try, Father, but I do not love perfectly.

My child, I want you to be intent on learning to love as I love you.
It is of paramount importance to Me.

Yes, Father. I want to do only what You desire. Here is my
heart—it is Yours. Fill it with Your love and do what is
necessary to teach me to love.

❦ THE SUPREMACY OF LOVE ❧

Three things will last forever—faith, hope, and love—and the greatest of these is love.

I CORINTHIANS 13:13

Love is the most God-like state of the soul. God is not faith or hope; God is love. The Eternal does not believe or anticipate, but he does love—he is love. Love is the life of the soul. It warms every vein and beats in every pulse.

DAVID THOMAS, IN *The Pulpit Commentary*

IN HIS FIRST LETTER TO the church at Corinth, the apostle Paul addressed a group of believers who were preoccupied with seeking and practicing the most prominent spiritual gifts. To help them maintain a balanced perspective, Paul encouraged the Corinthians to pursue "a more excellent way" (1 Corinthians 12:31, NKJV). The best way to minister to the body of Christ, he concluded, was to exercise the supreme virtue of love. Although he acknowledged the lasting value of faith and hope, even these would one day be eclipsed. For Paul to single out one virtue as the greatest, above all others, indicates that he had a firm conviction based on his own experience and his certainty of the heart of God. Categorically and boldly, he proclaimed that the highest, the loveliest, the pre-eminent virtue of all is love.

❧ THE PROMINENCE OF LOVE

1. To discover the heart of God and what He desires most for His children, we can examine His Word. What central theme is taught in each of the following Scriptures?

MARK 12:28-31 .... ❧

Love of God(ess) Elohim and Lord.
Love of the fellow human/neighbor.
To do both you must also love yourself.
Seek within yourself love by mirroring it
from the love of God back into yourself.
Love thyself or thou canst love thy neighbor
To love thy neighbor as much as you love yourself.

ROMANS 13:8-9 *Not subjective love. Objective Love!*

Love of self + leads with applied knowledge.
Love of others, brothers sisters
When you love yourself with jurisprudence
of knowledge of the commandments. To apply
Love *this knowledge with love and respect of*
Toward the self (being balanced) you obey the command to
other *love thy neighbor as thyself.*

1 CORINTHIANS 13:13 .... ❧

1 CORINTHIANS 16:14 .... ❧

2. Of all the commands in the Bible and among all the great virtues, love reigns supreme. What do these passages communicate about why love is God's priority?

ROMANS 13:10 ··· ♫

1 CORINTHIANS 8:1-3 ······································ ♫

COLOSSIANS 3:14 ··· ♫

3. Our culture has given us many popular songs and sayings
   about the importance and beauty of love. List some of your
   favorite song titles or quotations, and then describe what kind
   of love is prized in our society.

———————————— ☙ ————————————

*Love being the most potent of forces, it is hardly surprising
that the most overwhelming experiences of life should
be those of being in love—first with God and then with
another human being.*

There is no trick of a magician or spell of a witch doctor, no drug or mesmerism or bribery or torture or coercion that can compare in power with the force for change unleashed in the human breast through the touch of love. Love is the greatest of teachers, for there is no authority more compelling, no power more hypnotically transfixing, no counsel more wise, no message we are more longing to hear, no other master for whom it is easier to give up absolutely everything in order to follow and obey.[1]

MIKE MASON

THE HIGHEST LOVE

4.　The world tends to glorify relational and physical love. But the greatest love, which Paul extolled, is from a rarely used word in the Greek language, *agape*. It describes "a love that is based on the deliberate choice of the one who loves rather than the worthiness of the one who is loved."[2] How do the following verses characterize this kind of love?

PSALM 145:8-9 ⸱⸱⸱

JEREMIAH 31:3 ⸱⸱⸱

JOHN 3:16-17 ....

1 CORINTHIANS 13:4-7 ....

---

*God, who needs nothing, loves into existence wholly
superfluous creatures in order that He may love and perfect
them. . . . If I may dare the biological image, God is a
"host" who deliberately creates His own parasites; causes us
to be that we may exploit and "take advantage of" Him.
Herein is love. This is the diagram of Love Himself, the
inventor of all loves.[3]*   C. S. LEWIS

5. Agape love is self-sacrificing, desiring the best for another.
   How has God demonstrated this kind of love to the world?
   How has His unconditional love shaped your life?

❧ THOUGHTS AND REFLECTIONS FROM AN OLDER WOMAN

Some of my favorite old love songs are by Irving Berlin: "I'll Be Loving You Always" and "How Deep Is the Ocean." I grew up listening to Elvis Presley sing "Love Me Tender," and many times I would find myself humming, "What the World Needs Now Is Love, Sweet Love." Browning's poetic stanza, "How do I love thee? Let me count the ways," Tennyson's declaration, "'Tis better to have loved and lost, than never to have loved at all," and the saying "Love makes the world go round" captured my attention as a young girl.

I remember watching the Academy Awards one year when an actress was so overcome with emotion as she received an Oscar that she repeatedly cried, "You *like* me!" It is, indeed, a precious gift to be loved, wanted, and accepted.

Throughout history the incalculable value of love has been proclaimed in every art form and culture—personally, privately, and publicly. Certainly the Scriptures address the whole scope of love. Sexual love in the context of marriage is blessed by God; love between friends is prized; and agape love is presented as the highest and best to achieve.

C. S. Lewis offers a unique insight into this special agape love when he portrays God as the host who actively invites and welcomes His "parasitic" children to cling to and depend upon Him. The connotation of the word *parasite* is usually negative because a parasite can ultimately destroy its host. There are, however, a few positive synonyms for the word *parasite*—*follower* and *attendant*—which perfectly describe those who choose to hold fast to the Lord

God. Far from destroying this loving Host, God's children bring Him pleasure when they acknowledge and accept His kind invitation to be fed, protected, and nurtured by Him.

God has demonstrated the highest love, for in Christ's sacrifice He has accepted His dependent followers unconditionally. In this beautiful context of agape love, the "parasite" embraces faith, experiences hope, and receives eternal life. What an extremely gracious Host is our God, who generously imparts His love to all who desire to live with Him. In loving and clinging to Him, we can experience the greatest love that life has to offer.

We know but little now about the conditions of the life that is to come. But what is certain is that Love must last. God, the Eternal God, is Love. Covet, therefore, that everlasting gift, that one thing which it is certain is going to stand, that one coinage which will be current in the Universe when all the other coinages of all the nations of the world shall be useless and unhonored. You will give yourselves to many things; give yourself first to Love.[4]

HENRY DRUMMOND

LOVE IMPARTED

6. As you review this chapter, ask the Lord what He wants you to learn concerning the supremacy of love. Is there a verse on which you need to meditate or a teaching about which you need to pray so that love can begin to dwell in your heart in a

more powerful way? Write down your thoughts and pray for God's love to invade your heart and teach you about what you personally need to become a woman who loves.

⚜ SCRIPTURE MEMORY

1 CORINTHIANS 13:13—*Three things will last forever—faith, hope, and love—and the greatest of these is love.*

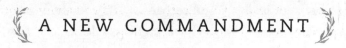

CHAPTER 2

A NEW COMMANDMENT

*Now I am giving you a new commandment: Love each other. Just as
I have loved you, you should love each other. Your love for one another
will prove to the world that you are my disciples.*

JOHN 13:34-35

*So new a type of love is given that, as the Greek expositors generally
have urged, there is a deeper intensity in the love than can be found
in the Mosaic principle, "Love thy neighbour as thyself." In this
commandment, which embraces the whole law, self-love is assumed,
and is made the standard for the love of neighbour. This [command],
on the other hand, would be based on a new principle, and measured
by a higher standard, and even mean more than love of self altogether.
Christ's love to his disciples was self-abandoning, self-sacrificing love.*

H. R. REYNOLDS, IN *The Pulpit Commentary*

A FEW HOURS BEFORE JESUS was betrayed, He was with His
disciples in the upper room. After Jesus had washed their feet,
they sat down to eat. During the course of the meal, Jesus pre-
dicted that one of them would betray Him. Soon after this pro-
nouncement, Judas left the room, and Jesus spoke these words to
those who remained: "Dear children, I will be with you only a
little longer. . . . So now I am giving you a new commandment"
(John 13:33-34). Only on His last night with His disciples did
Jesus share this new directive. On the eve of leaving His faithful

followers, His final words took on the utmost importance. In essence He was saying, "You've been with Me for three years, and you know the commands given from Moses, but now as I depart I am giving you a new commandment. Listen to it carefully because this command is essential for the establishment and unity of the church and for your witness to the world."

A SACRIFICIAL LOVE

1. Jesus raised the standard concerning how we are to love one another. He left a model of how to love, and He asked that His disciples love in the same way. As you read the verses below, record how Jesus exemplified the heart of love.

EPHESIANS 5:1-2

PHILIPPIANS 2:5-8

1 PETER 2:18-25

1 JOHN 3:16 ··

2. Jesus constantly demonstrated His love for others. As you read the following passages, write down your observations in the columns provided, stating how and to whom Jesus showed compassion.

Scripture	Who Was Involved?	What Did Jesus Do?
Matthew 9:35-38		
Matthew 15:32-37		
John 8:1-11		
John 13:1-17		

Perhaps most humbling of all Jesus' compassionate acts before Calvary was the foot-washing episode in the upper room, recorded in John 13:3–15. This event occurred just prior to the command to love one another. It is difficult for us to comprehend the Lord of Heaven taking on the role of a servant, but he did what was customary in Eastern homes for servants to do—wash the dusty feet of guests. One would assume that others of the group should have offered to perform this service. But Jesus' love was on display in this act of humility. . . . He gave himself completely to them. He could have demanded his rights and could have called on one of them to perform this humbling service, but he chose to serve them. And, remarkably, he chose to include Judas, who had already sold out to the devil.[1] WILLIAM M. FLETCHER

3. Jesus not only asked the disciples in the upper room to love as He loved, but He asks us to do the same. How do you react to being asked to love as Jesus loves?

⚜ LOVING OTHERS

4. The new command focuses on a specific group of people. In the following passages, Jesus speaks to His disciples and John

writes to the church. What are their instructions regarding how and whom to love?

JOHN 13:34-35 ·· ௸

1 JOHN 4:7 ·· ௸

5. Jesus taught that there are others we are to love. What do these Scriptures tell us about whom else we are to love and how we are to relate to them?

LUKE 6:27-36 ·· ௸

LUKE 10:25-37 ·· ௸

—————— ∽ ——————

*To be a disciple means that we deliberately identify
ourselves with God's interests in other people. Jesus says,
"That ye love one another, as I have loved you. . . ."
The expression of Christian character is not good doing,
but Godlikeness: If the Spirit of God has transformed you
within, you will exhibit Divine characteristics in your life,
not good human characteristics. God's life in us expresses
itself as God's life, not as a human life trying to be godly.[2]*

OSWALD CHAMBERS

6. One recurring theme that Jesus modeled and emphasized in
His teaching on love is the idea of sacrificially laying down
one's life for friends and others. What are some ways of laying
down one's life for the good of someone else?

❦ THOUGHTS AND REFLECTIONS
FROM AN OLDER WOMAN

It is significant that John 13 begins with the statement, "Before
the Passover celebration, Jesus knew that his hour had come
to leave this world and return to his Father. He had loved
his disciples during his ministry on earth, and now he loved
them to the very end" (verse 1). His first act in *showing the full
extent of His love* was to wash their feet. His last act was dying on

the cross for our redemption. Jesus was humbly willing to offer Himself as a servant, obediently sacrificing Himself for others (friends or enemies), graciously demonstrating His love to the full extent. To love as Jesus loved is to keep a towel wrapped around our waists so that we are ready to bow down and "wash their feet" as needed.

One day I went into the kitchen to prepare a cup of tea, and I asked my husband if he wanted some too. He thought for a moment and then replied, "Actually, I'd like a cup of hot chocolate." Standing at the stove (without a "towel" around my waist) I replied, "Well, hon, if you want hot chocolate, you'll have to fix it yourself. I only have time to make tea."

All of a sudden I had become a Levite rushing down the road past a man in need—with no time in my schedule for anything extra. Sure, I would serve, but only when it was convenient and as long as it didn't interrupt my agenda. Certainly, Jack was not lying beside the road wounded, but my response to him mirrored the attitude of the priest in our Lord's parable of the Good Samaritan (see Luke 10:25-37).

This new commandment is hard and is a continual challenge—to love sacrificially, humbly, and selflessly. To love in this way, I must always be conscious of the "towel." For me, putting on the towel means surrendering my heart to do whatever the Lord asks and then being watchful, ready to love and serve whoever crosses my path. The towel should be so much a part of my life that I "wear" it always, a reminder to give the full extent of my love just as Jesus did.

"A cup of hot chocolate? Certainly! Coming right up."

——————————— ೧෨ ———————————

We instinctively know that love leads to commitment, so
we look away when we see a beggar. We might have to pay
if we look too closely and care too deeply. Loving means
losing control of our schedule, our money, and our time.
When we love we cease to be the master and become a
servant.[3]　　　　　　　　　　　　　　PAUL E. MILLER

❧ LOVE IMPARTED

7.　As you review this chapter, ask the Lord what He wants you
to learn concerning Jesus' new commandment. Is there a verse
on which you need to meditate or a teaching about which you
need to pray so that love can begin to dwell in your heart in a
more powerful way? Write down your thoughts and pray for
God's love to invade your heart and teach you about what you
personally need to become a woman who loves.

❧ SCRIPTURE MEMORY

JOHN 13:34-35—*Now I am giving you a new commandment: Love*
each other. Just as I have loved you, you should love each other.
Your love for one another will prove to the world that you are my
disciples.

CHAPTER 3

THE SOURCE OF LOVE

God showed how much he loved us by sending his one and only Son into the world so that we might have eternal life through him. This is real love—not that we loved God, but that he loved us and sent his Son as a sacrifice to take away our sins.

Dear friends, since God loved us that much, we surely ought to love each other.

I JOHN 4:9-11

The springs of love are in God, not in us. It is absurd to look for the love of God in our hearts naturally, it is only there when it has been shed abroad in our hearts by the Holy Spirit.

OSWALD CHAMBERS, *My Utmost for His Highest*

THE NEW COMMANDMENT TO LOVE as Jesus loved us is a compelling charge—a daunting challenge that seems almost impossible to fulfill. I am not naturally compassionate. I don't see that I have any extra time to give to the wounded by the roadside. I don't like being interrupted, something that happened to Jesus all the time. He loved the lost, the sinful, the grieving. He fed people and washed dusty feet. Am I supposed to do this too? After all, He was God Incarnate; how can I be expected to love as He did? But because I have received God's love, I will be able to love with *His* love. This is the way God provides for those who desire to obey His commands. Thankfully, all our springs find their source in Him.

❧ GOD'S LOVE TO US

1. Loving others sacrificially is not something we can do in our
    own strength. What do the following verses communicate
    about God's love for us and how we can receive it?

    ROMANS 5:5-11.. ✍

    EPHESIANS 2:4-7 .... ✍

    1 JOHN 4:7-16.. ✍

2. Once we receive Jesus Christ as our Savior and Lord, our lives
    are transformed. What do these verses teach about some of the
    changes that occur when the Holy Spirit fills our hearts with
    His love?

    2 CORINTHIANS 5:14-17................................... ✍

EPHESIANS 3:14-19 ··

1 PETER 1:22-23 ··

——————— ⌇ ———————

Without Christ we should not know God, we could not call upon Him, nor come to Him. But without Christ we also would not know our brother, nor could we come to him. The way is blocked by our own ego. Christ opened up the way to God and to our brother. Now Christians can live with one another in peace; they can love and serve one another; they can become one. But they can continue to do so only by way of Jesus Christ. Only in Jesus Christ are we one, only through Him are we bound together. To eternity He remains the one Mediator.[1] DIETRICH BONHOEFFER

3. Personally accepting Jesus' sacrifice on the cross ushers in new spiritual birth; old things pass away (see 2 Corinthians 5:17). Describe some of the ways in which your acceptance of Christ has changed your life.

⚜ GOD'S LOVE IN US

4. Once God's love is, as Oswald Chambers puts it, "shed abroad
    in our hearts," the Holy Spirit begins to work in our lives.
    What insights can you find in these passages about how God
    empowers us in learning to love?

    JOHN 17:20-26 ·

    PHILIPPIANS 2:13 ·

    1 THESSALONIANS 3:12-13 ·

    1 THESSALONIANS 4:9-10 ·

5. God is at work in us to conform us to the image of Christ
    (see Romans 8:29), but it is necessary that we have responsive

hearts. What do the following verses tell us about how we are to grow in love?

JOHN 14:21-24 ....

JOHN 15:9-10 ....

1 JOHN 5:1-3 ....

———————— ⟡ ————————

*When God hath given us of his own Spirit and love,
so that we in our measure come to love like God, then
we know that "we dwell in him, and he in us." There
is a loving and abiding intercommunion. We, being in
full sympathy with God, must needs yearn to pour forth
ourselves to others, as God hath given himself to us. And
this outgoing of ourselves to our brother is a sure pledge of
God being in us, and we in him.*[2]   C. CLEMANCE

6. It is encouraging to know that the Lord is at work in our lives teaching us to love. How does this knowledge affect your attitude toward loving others?

❧ THOUGHTS AND REFLECTIONS FROM AN OLDER WOMAN

One of my favorite hymns is Charles Wesley's "And Can It Be That I Should Gain?" Wesley wrote, "Died He for me, who caused His pain? For me, who Him to death pursued? Amazing love! How can it be that Thou, my God, shouldst die for me?"[3] When the full extent of God's love for me begins to flood my life, I realize that God's love is not only amazing but overwhelming. The great love He demonstrated at the cross on my behalf humbles me and draws me to Himself. How can I ever adequately express my gratitude?

I think Jesus tells me simply, *Cynthia, the love that I have given you, I want you to give to others. You are not to try to love with the little love that dwells in your heart, but if you will keep My commands, then I will manifest Myself to you, and I will teach you and cause you to abound in love. Stay close to the Source. It is My love that I want you to impart. I'm not asking you to do something that is impossible. In fact, what I'm asking you to do is really simple: Accept the love I have for you; allow Me to live in you so that I can teach you how to love. Let Me fill you with My love, My life, My power. In this way you will begin to experience the incomparable blessing of knowing Me and what it is really like to love as I love.*

"My dear, dear friends, if God loved us like this, we certainly ought to love each other." (1 John 4:11, MSG)

From God's other known attributes we may learn much about His love. We can know, for instance, that because God is self-existent, His love had no beginning; because He is eternal, His love can have no end; because He is infinite, it has no limit; because He is holy, it is the quintessence of all spotless purity; because He is immense, His love is an incomprehensibly vast, bottomless, shoreless sea before which we kneel in joyful silence and from which the loftiest eloquence retreats confused and abashed.[4]

A. W. TOZER

LOVE IMPARTED

7. As you review this chapter, ask the Lord what He wants you to learn concerning the Source of your love. Is there a verse on which you need to meditate or a teaching about which you need to pray so that His love can begin to dwell in your heart in a more powerful way? Write down your thoughts and pray for God's love to invade your heart and teach you about what you personally need to become a woman who loves.

❦ SCRIPTURE MEMORY

1 JOHN 4:9-11—*God showed how much he loved us by sending his one and only Son into the world so that we might have eternal life through him. This is real love—not that we loved God, but that he loved us and sent his Son as a sacrifice to take away our sins.*

    Dear friends, since God loved us that much, we surely ought to love each other.

BEARING FRUIT

*I am the vine, you are the branches. He who abides in Me, and I in
him, bears much fruit; for without Me you can do nothing.*

JOHN 15:5, NKJV

*His purpose is not that you will do more for Him but that you will choose
to be more with Him. Only by abiding can you enjoy the most rewarding
friendship with God and experience the greatest abundance for His glory.*

*To abide means to remain, to stay closely connected, to settle in for
the long term. With this picture Jesus is showing the disciples how an
ongoing, vital connection with Him will directly determine the amount
of His supernatural power at work in their lives.*

BRUCE WILKINSON, *Secrets of the Vine*

JESUS DEPICTED HIMSELF AS THE Vine, the Source from
which His followers draw strength, nourishment, and the ability
to bear fruit. In describing believers as branches, Jesus portrayed
a living and lasting relationship of commitment to Him. It was in
this context of abiding that He repeated the new commandment,
to love one another as He has loved us (see John 15:12). The best
choice we can make in order to fulfill this commandment is to stay
closely connected to Him. The result of abiding is the precious
fruit of Christlikeness. If we do not abide in Him, Jesus makes it
clear that we can do nothing—we will bear no fruit, and we will

eventually wither into lifelessness. To love the Lord and keep His commands, abiding is essential.

⚘ THE FLESH AND THE SPIRIT

1. The choices and decisions we make daily determine the kind of fruit that our lives will produce. Fill in the columns below as you read these passages concerning fruit bearing.

Scripture	Fruit of Our Sinful Nature	Fruit of the Holy Spirit
Galatians 5:16-26		
Ephesians 5:1-10		
James 3:13-18		

In the flesh, or our depraved nature, there is lust or desire for sinful gratification in some form or another. How are we to be delivered from this, so that it shall not be fulfilled? The way is positively to follow the leading of the Spirit. The idea is not that we are to follow the tendencies of our renewed nature. That is missing the personal aspect of the leading. The Spirit, indeed, renews the nature, and excites within it holy desires which seek for gratification. But the Spirit gives personal guiding, especially in and by the reason and conscience in connection with the Word. And as a Guide he is all-sufficient. He is an internal Guide. He throws all the light that we need upon the character of desires and actions, upon the path of duty.[1]

R. FINLAYSON

2. Certainly the flesh lusts against the Spirit. What insight and encouragement to walk in the Spirit can you find in these verses concerning our old sin nature?

ROMANS 8:1-5 ....

GALATIANS 5:24-25 ....

To be dead to a thing is a strong expression denoting that it has no influence over us. A man that is dead is uninfluenced and unaffected by the affairs of this life. He is insensible to sounds, and tastes, and pleasures; to the hum of business, to the voice of friendship, and to all the scenes of commerce, gaiety, and ambition. When it is said, therefore, that a Christian is dead *to sin, the sense is, that it has lost its influence over him; he is not subject to it; he is in regard to that, as the man in the grave is to the busy scenes and cares of this life.[2]*   ALBERT BARNES

3. The Scriptures exhort us to be wise and understanding. How would you summarize the most important truths we need to understand and apply in our lives in order to produce the spiritual fruit of love?

❧ THE VINE AND THE BRANCHES

4. When Jesus was sharing with His disciples on His last night, He left them (and us) a clear picture of what is necessary to be His follower and to bear fruit. You have already read parts of John 15, but there is much in this chapter that you can study from different perspectives. Read John 15:1-17 and write down the ways in which Jesus' use of the vine imagery teaches us about bearing the fruit of love.

5. Jesus taught that a branch cannot bear fruit by itself. Describe any times in your life when you have tried to bear the fruit of love without abiding in Christ.

❧ THOUGHTS AND REFLECTIONS FROM AN OLDER WOMAN

Few words have had more impact in my life than Jesus' statement, "Apart from me you can do nothing" (John 15:5, NIV). Many years ago, after meditating on this verse, I thought, *I don't want to spend my life doing nothing, so if it takes abiding to do* something, *then that is what I'll do for the rest of my life.* Struggling with the busyness of life and my own selfish desires, I have tried to be a branch that remains in the Vine. For me, staying connected to Christ means prayerfully reading His Word daily, memorizing key verses that I really need, and having an ongoing dialogue with the living God throughout the day.

One thing I've learned is that consistent abiding enables me to persevere through pruning—a necessary tool for fruit bearing. Having to let go of dreams, people, the demands of my flesh, and my poor strategies for living are all a part of pruning. Pruning is thinning out, removing, detaching, cleansing—all of it to help me develop and become a sturdy branch, strongly rooted in and connected to the Vine. As I mature, my desire is to draw more and more nourishment from the Lord, to grow in intimacy, and, I hope, to begin to bear much fruit in my desire to love as He loved.

In practical terms, fruit represents good works—a thought, attitude, or action of ours that God values because it glorifies Him. The fruit from your life is how God receives His due honor on earth. That's why Jesus declares, "By this My Father is glorified, that you bear much fruit" (John 15:8).

You bear inner fruit when you allow God to nurture in you a new, Christlike quality: "The fruit of the Spirit is love, joy, peace, longsuffering, kindness, goodness, faithfulness, gentleness, self-control" (Galatians 5:22).

You bear outward fruit when you allow God to work through you to bring Him glory.[3]   BRUCE WILKINSON

⚘ LOVE IMPARTED

6. As you review this chapter, ask the Lord what He wants you to learn concerning bearing the fruit of abiding. Is there a verse on which you need to meditate or a teaching about which you need to pray so that His love can begin to dwell in your heart in a more powerful way? Write down your thoughts and pray for God's love to invade your heart and teach you about what you personally need to become a woman who loves.

⚘ SCRIPTURE MEMORY

JOHN 15:5 —*I am the vine, you are the branches. He who abides in Me, and I in him, bears much fruit; for without Me you can do nothing. (NKJV)*

CHAPTER 5

THE CHARACTER OF LOVE

Love is patient and kind. Love is not jealous or boastful or proud or rude. It does not demand its own way. It is not irritable, and it keeps no record of being wronged. It does not rejoice about injustice but rejoices whenever the truth wins out. Love never gives up, never loses faith, is always hopeful, and endures through every circumstance.

I CORINTHIANS 13:4-7

Love is the badge and character of Christianity.

DONALD S. WHITNEY, *Ten Questions to Diagnose Your Spiritual Health*

IN THE RENOWNED CHAPTER 13 of Paul's first letter to the Corinthian church, we find the beautiful, challenging, and extraordinary description of love. It is in defining the "more excellent way" (see 1 Corinthians 12:31, NIV) that Paul specifically characterizes the many facets of love. After reading this passage, we come away realizing that love is no longer an ethereal concept that only gives us "warm fuzzies." The Word depicts love in all its earthly reality. This love reacts and responds to relationships and circumstances on a distinctively spiritual plane. This love will outlast all spiritual gifts. This love is not hypocritical or self-serving. This love is from above, given to us to put into practice in our world. It is to be so evident that all who meet us will experience its outworking. It is to be the badge of the Christian.

❧ LOVE DEFINED

1. Throughout history, many people have attempted to define love. Study Paul's bold statements in 1 Corinthians 13:1-3. Why do you think that the exercise of spiritual gifts and acts of sacrificial service are worth nothing from God's perspective if they are done without love?

2. To create a character sketch of love and its opposite, list all the words Paul used in 1 Corinthians 13:4-5 to define what love is and what love is not. Use a dictionary and at least one other Bible translation to define these qualities.

    a. Love *is* . . .

    b. Love *is not* . . .

3. Which of the qualities Paul described do you most appreciate in others? Why?

⸎

*Love suffers for a long time. Our modern "throw-away"
society encourages us to get rid of people in our lives
who are difficult to get along with, whether they are
friends, family or acquaintances. Yet this attitude runs
in complete contrast to the love described by Paul. True
love puts up with people who would be easier to give
up on.[1]*

4. Paul further defined love in 1 Corinthians 13:6-7 by how it is
   expressed. Record these distinguishing characteristics.

   a. Love *does not . . .*

   b. Love *does . . .*

5. Which of these characteristics challenges you the most in
   expressing love? Why?

6. After describing the character of love in the first seven verses of chapter 13, Paul shifted to the transcendent nature of love. In verses 8-13, he clarified that the spiritual gifts, practical as they are to the body of Christ, are temporal. Read 1 Corinthians 13:8-13 and summarize the case Paul made for love being the "most excellent way."

The argument is, that we ought not to seek so anxiously that which is so imperfect and obscure, and which must soon vanish away; but we should rather seek that love which is permanent, expanding, and eternal.[2]

ALBERT BARNES

7. Paul's exhortation depicts the transforming nature of love. Take a moment to examine how this Christlike love is becoming evident in your life. What specific quality in your character needs the most work?

⚜ THOUGHTS AND REFLECTIONS FROM AN OLDER WOMAN

"THY LOVE"

The love that gives
no thought to *me*,
but willingly yields
its all to Thee—
O Lord, bestow
deep in my heart
Thy gracious love
ne'er to depart.

CYNTHIA HEALD

How many of you will join me in reading this chapter
[1 Corinthians 13] once a week for the next three
months? A man did that once and it changed his
whole life. Will you do it? It is for the greatest thing
in the world. You might begin by reading it every day,
especially the verses which describe the perfect character.
"Love suffereth long, and is kind; love envieth not; love
vaunteth not itself." Get these ingredients into your life.
Then everything that you do is eternal. It is worth doing.
It is worth giving time to. No man can become a saint in
his sleep; and to fulfill the condition required demands
a certain amount of prayer and meditation and time,
just as improvement in any direction, bodily or mental,
requires preparation and care. Address yourselves to that

one thing; at any cost have this transcendent character exchanged for yours.[3]

HENRY DRUMMOND

LOVE IMPARTED

8. As you review this chapter, ask the Lord what He wants you to learn concerning the character of love. Is there a verse on which you need to meditate or a teaching about which you need to pray so that His love can begin to dwell in your heart in a more powerful way? Write down your thoughts and pray for God's love to invade your heart and teach you about what you personally need to become a woman who loves.

SCRIPTURE MEMORY

1 CORINTHIANS 13:4-7—*Love is patient and kind. Love is not jealous or boastful or proud or rude. It does not demand its own way. It is not irritable, and it keeps no record of being wronged. It does not rejoice about injustice but rejoices whenever the truth wins out. Love never gives up, never loses faith, is always hopeful, and endures through every circumstance.*

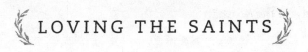 LOVING THE SAINTS

*Accept each other just as Christ has accepted you so that God will be
given glory.*
ROMANS 15:7

*When God was merciful, when He revealed Jesus Christ to us as our
Brother, when He won our hearts by His love, this was the beginning
of our instruction in divine love. When God was merciful to us, we
learned to be merciful with our brethren. When we received forgiveness
instead of judgment, we, too, were made ready to forgive our brethren.
What God did to us, we then owed to others. The more we received, the
more we were able to give; and the more meager our brotherly love, the
less were we living by God's mercy and love. Thus God Himself taught
us to meet one another as God has met us in Christ.*
DIETRICH BONHOEFFER, *Life Together*

SINCE LOVE IS THE SUPREME gift to receive and to give, Jesus
has commanded, not just recommended, that we love one another
as He has loved us. His love was sacrificial and selfless; this is the
kind of love we are to give to others. The good news is that the
source of our love is from God Himself, and it becomes ours as we
abide in Christ and obey His commands. Jesus wants His saints to
bear the fruit of love especially to the body of Christ, for it sends
a powerful message to the world that we belong to Him. This
body of believers is distinctive and knitted together according to

His purposes in order to accomplish His will in the church and ultimately in the world.

❧ THE BODY OF CHRIST

1. The Bible speaks of the children of God who compose His family as "saints." What distinguishing characteristics of this family or body of believers do you find in the following verses?

    1 CORINTHIANS 12:12-14 .... ✌

    EPHESIANS 2:19-22 .... ✌

    COLOSSIANS 1:15-18 .... ✌

2. The body of Christ is uniquely fashioned to work together. What insights can you find in the following passages about God's purpose for His body and how He has equipped it to function?

ROMANS 12:3-8··

1 CORINTHIANS 12:4-11································

EPHESIANS 4:11-16································

Christians are not independent of each other: they
should not seek to be so. *We are not the body of Christ*
individually, *but we are* collectively. *We are not set to*
stand alone, but with others. We can help others and
be helped ourselves. Another's work may be needful for
the success of ours, ours for the success of another's. One
supplies just what *the other lacks. So that if all supply*
what they can, the body becomes perfect in working.[1]

H. BREMNER

3. God equips each of His children with gifts so they can serve. As you have been a part of a body (church, Bible study, fellowship meeting), what one or two observations can you make concerning how different members build up one another?

❧ LOVE FOR THE BODY

4. Christ is the head of the body, and His Word describes how we should conduct ourselves with one another. What do the following Scriptures teach about how we are to relate within the body?

EPHESIANS 4:1-6 .... ❧

COLOSSIANS 3:14-15 .... ❧

1 PETER 4:7-11 .... ❧

5. All of these exhortations encourage us to express love for other Christians. Which verse or verses challenge you the most in terms of the command to love others? Why?

You love God as much as the one you love the least.[2]

JOHN J. HUGO

THOUGHTS AND REFLECTIONS FROM AN OLDER WOMAN

I am always amazed to see the body of Christ at work. There are those dear people who organize a variety of activities: Sunday school classes, vacation Bible school, short-term mission trips, neighborhood clean-up days. They enjoy the challenge; they have a great ability to motivate others to help; and they are good at seeing the overall picture. This is definitely a gift from the Holy Spirit to serve the church.

I do not have this gift. It would be extremely stressful for me to organize anything! I'm usually still having conversations with people after a church get-together when everyone else starts to clean up. I feel guilty, but then I think, *No, I feel called to sit here and talk to and encourage this person.* I don't need to feel guilty, though, because on those days when I'm not embroiled in conversation with someone, I'm eagerly helping with the cleanup. So I realize that although I'm eager to do my fair share, I'm not usually the first to start washing dishes.

It is encouraging to see how God has knit us together for the good of the whole body. Now, in order for me not to feel envious ("I'm not the committee chairman"), or guilty ("I'm not always the first to start washing dishes"), I need to understand that Christ is the head of the body and the Holy Spirit bestows the gifts as He purposes. It is *God's* church, not mine!

Essentially, what the Lord wants me to do above all else is to love other Christians fervently. In loving them, I am motivated to use my gift, and the body is blessed. When I do love and serve, I promote unity and God is glorified.

It all sounds good and right to love the body, but the church is composed of individuals who, for me, are not always easy to love *fervently*. I think Peter wrote from his own experience with the church when he said, "Most important of all, continue to show deep love for each other, for love covers a multitude of sins" (1 Peter 4:8). And the apostle John did not mince words—"And he has given us this command: Those who love God must also love their fellow believers" (1 John 4:21).

Again I'm reminded that love is the supreme gift and that loving the saints is really a matter of obeying Christ's command; it is a choice I must make if I say I love God.

How can I fulfill this command to love passionately, gently, and patiently? Perhaps I need to continually revisit the Vine, strengthening and deepening my connection to the Source as I take on the character of love.

> Sanctification means the impartation of the Holy qualities of Jesus Christ. It is His patience, His love, His holiness, His faith, His purity, His godliness, that is manifested in and through every sanctified soul.[3]
>
> OSWALD CHAMBERS

 ## LOVE IMPARTED

6. As you review this chapter, ask the Lord what He wants you to learn concerning loving the saints. Is there a verse on which you need to meditate or a teaching about which you need to pray so that His love can begin to dwell in your heart in a more powerful way? Write down your thoughts and pray for God's love to invade your heart and teach you about what you personally need to become a woman who loves.

 ## SCRIPTURE MEMORY

ROMANS 15:7—*Accept each other just as Christ has accepted you so that God will be given glory.*

CHAPTER 7

❧ LOVE IN ACTION ❧

Dear children, let us stop loving with words or lips alone, but let us love with actions and in truth.
I JOHN 3:18, WMS

Compliments and flatteries become not Christians; but the sincere expressions of sacred affection, and the services or labours of love, do.
MATTHEW HENRY, *Commentary on the Whole Bible*

STUDYING THE SCRIPTURES TO UNDERSTAND God's great love has shown us what supreme value God places on love. We have gotten glimpses of Jesus' love, of His compassion for others, of His love for us. His words on the night of His betrayal comprised truths straight from His heart to His close disciples. During that time, He shared a new command—a fitting admonition from the Son of God to His followers—"I want you to love one another as you have seen Me love." It is indeed an encouragement to read and study about this love, but it is not enough just to think about it or discuss it. This declaration demands action, not a weak verbal response. Love that actively demonstrates the sacrificial love of Christ is what the Lord desires.

❧ LOVING IN DEED

1. We have studied how Jesus showed compassion to others by ministering to them in tangible ways. What instruction and encouragement can you find in the following passages about how to express love?

   ROMANS 12:9-13 ·· ❧

   HEBREWS 13:1-3 ·· ❧

   1 JOHN 3:17-18 ·· ❧

2. There are innumerable ways that love can be conveyed to others. There are conditions, though, on the kind of love that should be communicated. What do the verses below reveal about what needs to be present in our lives when we minister to others?

   1 CORINTHIANS 13:1-3 ··· ❧

COLOSSIANS 3:17 ....

1 PETER 1:22 ....

3. Just because we do something good for someone doesn't necessarily mean that we have done it in a way that brings glory to God. What personal needs might underlie your attempts to love others for your own benefit instead of for God's glory?

When the self knows that it is already accepted, unconditionally, there is no need anymore for it to preoccupy itself with advancing its own claims or with trying to create the conditions that might make it worthy of being loved. As long as the self is consumed in the struggle to make itself lovely, it cannot love. First it must come to the end of its own resources, for the power to love derives purely and solely from the knowledge that one is

already loved in return. The energy for love flows not out of any effort, but simply from being loved.[1]   MIKE MASON

LOVING IN TRUTH

4. Truth incorporates authenticity, genuineness, righteousness, and integrity. Certainly our expressions of love should be genuine, but because all Christians have different abilities and are at various stages of maturity, the Scriptures address some of the concerns that can make it difficult to love in truth. Study what Paul taught in Romans 14:1–15:3 about relating to one another and write down his instructions.

5. Under the influence of the Holy Spirit, Paul wrote these words in Romans to avoid potential problems in the church. How do you see these same issues affecting the church today?

THOUGHTS AND REFLECTIONS FROM AN OLDER WOMAN

Essentially, love in action means laying down our lives. To lay down means to give up, to relinquish, to surrender. It means considering the needs of others above my own, proactively looking to see if my brothers or sisters are in need. It means walking in the Spirit so that I can listen to and obey His promptings to love.

How often I've been with people, listening to them tell what is happening in their lives, and when it's time for us to part, I give a quick hug and a smile and send them off. It's usually afterward that I realize there were several ways I could have expressed genuine love to them. Most importantly, I could have prayed with them—whatever their circumstances.

From this chapter, I come away with a deeper conviction to pray—for a fervent love, a sacred affection, a pure heart, a sensitivity to the needs of the saints, a tender spirit, a courteous manner. Perhaps as I pray and abide in Christ, then causing another to stumble will not be an issue in my life. Perhaps as I pray and abide in Christ, then the little I do will be done in truth and in the name of the Lord Jesus. Perhaps as I pray and abide in Christ, I will be able to lovingly and willingly lay down my life in countless ways—just as Jesus did for me.

This is how we've come to understand and experience love: Christ sacrificed his life for us. This is why we ought to live sacrificially for our fellow believers, and not just be out for ourselves. If you see some brother or sister in need and have the means to do something about it but turn a cold shoulder and do nothing, what happens to God's love? It disappears. And you made it disappear.

I JOHN 3:16-17, MSG

 LOVE IMPARTED

6. As you review this chapter, ask the Lord what He wants you to learn concerning how to love in deed and in truth. Is there a verse on which you need to meditate or a teaching about which you need to pray so that His love can begin to dwell in your heart in a more powerful way? Write down your thoughts and pray for God's love to invade your heart and teach you about what you personally need to become a woman who loves.

SCRIPTURE MEMORY

1 JOHN 3:18—*Dear children, let us stop loving with words or lips alone, but let us love with actions and in truth.* (WMS)

CHAPTER 8

❦ LOVE FORGIVES ❧

*Be gentle with one another, sensitive. Forgive one another as quickly
and thoroughly as God in Christ forgave you.*
EPHESIANS 4:32, MSG

*Given the reality of sin, love and forgiveness are inextricably bound
together. God is continually, literally, second-by-second covering our sin
under His Son's blood and forgiving us our sins. God cannot love us
unless He forgives us and cannot forgive us without a commitment to
love us. Love and forgiveness are equally bound together in all human
relationships. I cannot hope to ever love someone unless I am committed
to forgive him. I cannot hope to ever forgive him—that is, truly forgive
him—unless I know the rich, incomprehensible joy of being forgiven.*
DAN ALLENDER, *Bold Love*

FORGIVENESS RUNS COUNTER TO HUMAN nature. When we
have been hurt, we want others to feel the hurt that has stung us.
But if we are intent on learning to love as Jesus loved, then we
must embrace and practice the loving act of forgiveness. Jesus'
death made possible our forgiveness and reconciliation: "In Him
we have redemption through His blood, the forgiveness of sins,
according to the riches of His grace" (Ephesians 1:7, NKJV). Since
the Lord extended His grace and forgiveness to us, so must we
give grace and forgiveness to others—loving as He loved. The
"forgiveness" part of love is one of the facets of love that makes it

supreme. True love forgives—it pardons, bears no grudge, covers a multitude of sins, does not take into account a wrong suffered. Forgiveness is rarely easy, but it is always right.

GOD'S FORGIVENESS TO US

1. The obedient Suffering Servant, the Lord Jesus, was wounded for our transgressions. Record two or three of your primary impressions concerning the Lord's sacrifice as you meditate on the prophetic passage in Isaiah 53.

2. God's mercy to us is as high as the heavens are above the earth. What do the following passages reveal about how God views our sin?

    PSALM 103:10-14 . . . .

    PSALM 130:3-4 . . . .

3. Sometimes we feel justified in withholding forgiveness. But that is not the way God treats us. What can the following passages teach us about God's mercy and grace to us?

ISAIAH 43:25 ···

ROMANS 3:21-26 ··

COLOSSIANS 3:12-13 ···

4. Our reluctance to forgive might be an indication that we have not fully received God's pardon. How has your experience of God's forgiveness influenced your forgiveness of others?

———————— ❧ ————————

I sometimes hear people say, "I forgive him—I just don't want to have anything to do with him again." This statement always makes me think of the part of the Lord's Prayer that says, "forgive us our debts, as we also have forgiven our debtors" (Matt. 6:12). Therefore, I will often respond to this kind of statement by asking, "What would happen if God forgave you in exactly the same way you are forgiving this other person? To put it another way, how would you feel if you had just confessed your sin to the Lord and then heard his voice saying, 'I forgive you—I just don't want to have anything to do with you again'?" Most people quickly agree that they wouldn't feel the least bit forgiven. As Christians, we cannot overlook the direct relationship between God's forgiveness and our forgiveness.[1]

KEN SANDE

❦ OUR FORGIVENESS TO OTHERS

5. God asks us to rise above our human tendencies in responding to people who hurt us. How does God's Word in Romans 12:17-21 teach us to deal with others' iniquities in a Christlike way?

6. Unforgiveness can be so destructive to our own lives that Jesus adds a "P.S." to the Lord's Prayer to warn us about it (see Matthew 6:14-15). The writer of Proverbs asserted that "runaway emotions corrode the bones" (Proverbs 14:30, MSG). What did Jesus teach in the following passages about the importance of forgiving others?

MATTHEW 6:9-15 .... ⌇

MATTHEW 18:21-35 .... ⌇

7. Jesus' teaching on forgiveness places a clear and definite condition on our forgiving others. What are some ways in which an unforgiving spirit can affect your relationship with the Lord?

—————————— ⌇ ——————————

The person who accepts forgiveness becomes deeply aware of his own weakness and need. Pride is ruled out as we take our place as supplicants before the Lord. This basic attitude releases us from our tendency to become angry with, or judgmental of, others. . . . [We] are freed to respond as God does, with loving concern and forgiveness. It isn't that God will not forgive the unforgiving. It is simply that the unforgiving lack the humble attitude that both permits them to accept forgiveness and frees them to extend forgiveness.[2]

LAWRENCE O. RICHARDS

❦ THOUGHTS AND REFLECTIONS
   FROM AN OLDER WOMAN

We are not to take lightly the Scripture that asks us to put away bitterness, wrath, and anger. If we don't relinquish bitterness, this strong emotion can destroy us from within.

I have come to understand that forgiving others is first and foremost for *my* good. Releasing others frees me from the devastating effects of holding onto anger and hurt. Whether the other person receives my forgiveness is not the major issue; what is important is that I extend forgiveness in obedience to the Lord.

I believe that the Lord loves me with a love that seeks only what is ultimately best for me. Because I love the Lord and desire to please Him, I want to do what He asks. As a forgiven child, I know that my heavenly Father will take vengeance and repay those who deserve it. Forgiveness does not mean that the perpetrator goes free; it means that the *forgiver* is free and that God will justly deal with those who have caused pain.

Forgiveness forged by love can radically change the forgiver. In this act of obedience I let go of the *me* who hurts, who wants to retaliate, who desires the other person to suffer as I have suffered. When I forgive, something extraordinary begins to take root in my soul, something fresh and new, something that makes me feel I am somehow stronger. For once I have done something that is counter to my *self* and though it doesn't seem logical, I know in my heart that it is right.

Could it be that the Lord God knows best? Could it be that to love and to forgive others blesses and enlarges the heart and soul of the lover and forgiver? And could it be that when we obey the

Lord's command to love as He loved, to forgive as He forgave, that we receive abundantly more than the little that we are asked to give?

> Forgiveness is not a feeling. Neither is it simply trying to forget the bad things done to us. It is an act of the will and heart. It is giving a person something they have not earned the right to have—pardon. Forgiveness acknowledges that we have been wronged but it goes beyond that and extends mercy.
>
> Sometimes forgiveness is a process. If we have been deeply hurt, it takes time for the wound to heal. In this case forgiveness acts as a continual cleansing of the wound so that it can heal properly. As we think about a person who has hurt us or sinned against us, feelings of resentment and emotional pain well up. Then we must reaffirm our commitment to forgive them. It is not that the first act of forgiveness was invalid, but that an ongoing process may be necessary until we are completely healed.[3]
>
> FLOYD MCCLUNG

🌿 LOVE IMPARTED

8. As you review this chapter, ask the Lord what He wants you to learn concerning forgiveness. Is there a verse on which you need to meditate or a teaching about which you need to pray so that His love can begin to dwell in your heart in a more powerful way? Write down your thoughts and pray for God's love to invade your heart and teach you about what you personally need to become a woman who loves.

SCRIPTURE MEMORY

EPHESIANS 4:32—*Be gentle with one another, sensitive. Forgive one another as quickly and thoroughly as God in Christ forgave you. (MSG)*

CHAPTER 9

❧ LOVE RECONCILES ❧

If you are in the act of worship and become aware that your actions have caused hurt, anger, resentment, or wounded feelings in another, your awareness requires initiative. Stop your acts of worship and make your best effort to restore peace and friendship by humbling yourself and accepting responsibility for the effects of your actions. Then continue your worship.
MATTHEW 5:23-24, PARAPHRASE BY DAVE LEGG, *Relational Healing Workbook*

We must not bring malice and hatred into the temple of the Lord; we cannot worship aright while we cherish wrath in our heart. For he is love, and the unloving cannot serve him acceptably. He will not accept the offerings of those who live in strife. Malice and envy rob the gift of all its value. Forgiveness of injuries, sorrow for our own offences, the humble petition for pardon from any whom we may have offended, is a sacrifice well pleasing unto God.
B. C. CAFFIN, IN *The Pulpit Commentary*

RESTORATION AND UNITY ARE OF supreme importance to God, who went all the way to the cross to reconcile us to Himself and thereby to one another. A forgiving heart desires to remove any hindrance that might exist in a relationship. When we worship the Lord, He looks for a pure and loving heart behind our offering.

Desire for unity, a willingness to humble ourselves, and a merciful heart honor and please the Lord.

Reconciliation involves acceptance, deference, peacemaking, and restoring harmony. Psalm 133:1 says, "Behold, how good and how pleasant it is for brethren to dwell together in unity" (NKJV). It is the good and pleasant—a reconciled body of believers—that love promotes.

❧ THE CALL OF RECONCILIATION

1. If the body of Christ is to function as God desires, harmony among its members is vital. What do the following Scriptures teach about our responsibility in fostering unity?

    2 CORINTHIANS 5:17-21 .... ❧

    PHILIPPIANS 2:1-3 .... ❧

    HEBREWS 10:24-25 .... ❧

Love works wisely and gently in a soul where he wills it, powerfully extinguishing short temper, envy, and all passions of anger and self-pity, bringing into the soul in their place the virtues of patience, mildness, peaceability, and warmth toward one's fellow Christians.[1]

WALTER HILTON

2. The writer of Hebrews exhorted Christians to "consider one another in order to stir up love and good works" (10:24, NKJV) within the body. What are some ways in which you might "stir up" love and good works to maintain harmony in your community of believers?

THE PRACTICE OF RECONCILIATION

3. In the Sermon on the Mount, Jesus identified our personal tendencies to be critical of others while overlooking our own faults. What instruction did Jesus give in Matthew 7:1-5 that can help us in practicing reconciliation?

Thus the passage as a whole does not say that we never ought to try to remove such "motes," but that this is monstrous and almost impossible so long as we ourselves have a fault of so much magnitude as censoriousness.[2]

A. LUKYN WILLIAMS

4. Because hurts and misunderstandings will occur within the body of Christ, the Scriptures teach us how to restore relationships. As you study the following verses, fill in the appropriate columns.

Scripture	Method of Dealing with the Offense	Person Responsible for Reconciliation
Matthew 5:21-24		
Matthew 18:15-17		
Galatians 6:1-5		

1 Peter 4:8		

Although it is often best simply to overlook the sins of others, there will be times when doing so only prolongs alienation and encourages them to continue acting in a hurtful manner. If you know that someone has something against you, go to that person and talk about it even before you worship God. Moreover, if another person's sins are dishonoring God, damaging your relationship, hurting others, or hurting that person, one of the most loving and helpful things you can do is to lovingly show that sinner where there is a need for change. With God's help and the right words (including your own confession), such a conversation will often lead to restored peace and stronger relationships.[3]

KEN SANDE

5. Peacekeeping can be a strong preventive against the need for reconciliation. What are some of the truths in these Scriptures that can help us keep the peace?

ZECHARIAH 8:16-17 .... ᕗ

EPHESIANS 4:29 .... ᕗ

1 PETER 3:8-12 .... ᕗ

————————— ᥫᩚ —————————

*Therefore, spiritual love proves itself in that everything it
says and does commends Christ. It will not seek to move
others by all too personal, direct influence, by impure
interference in the life of another. It will not take pleasure
in pious, human fervor and excitement. It will rather meet
the other person with the clear Word of God and be ready
to leave him alone with this Word for a long time, willing
to release him again in order that Christ may deal with
him. It will respect the line that has been drawn between
him and us by Christ, and it will find full fellowship
with him in the Christ who alone binds us together.*[4]

DIETRICH BONHOEFFER

6. Reconciliation is a sacred act of love and obedience. What hindrances to reconciliation can you identify in your life?

THOUGHTS AND REFLECTIONS FROM AN OLDER WOMAN

Reconciliation certainly is a sacred act of love and obedience. My initial response to conflict is to hide and hope the discord will disappear. I will rationalize that perhaps the other person really wasn't aware of or hurt by my insensitivity. But I have found that if someone's name keeps slipping into my thoughts while praying or worshiping, then I know I need to go to that person and be reconciled.

I have learned that when I obediently and humbly ask for forgiveness and for restoration, I sense a deeper intimacy with the Lord and usually a stronger bond with the one I offended. But there will be times when the one offended does not want to be restored. A verse that has helped me concerning difficult relationships is Romans 12:18: "Do all that you can to live in peace with everyone." I am responsible to do my part, but I am not accountable for the response of the other person.

It is the prompting of the Lord that I depend on to know when to overlook an offense or when to go to someone to ask forgiveness. I like what Charles H. Brent observed: "Intercessory prayer might be defined as loving our neighbor on our knees."[5] Through abiding in the Word and spending time in prayer, I can look for God's faithful leading to indicate how I should respond in restoring a relationship and how to speak only what is necessary for the building up of the body. Then my part is to obey lovingly and do all I can to uphold what is good and pleasant in the body of Christ.

❧ LOVE IMPARTED

7. As you review this chapter, ask the Lord what He wants you to learn concerning reconciliation. Is there a verse on which you need to meditate or a teaching about which you need to pray so that His love can begin to dwell in your heart in a more powerful way? Write down your thoughts and pray for God's love to invade your heart and teach you about what you personally need to become a woman who loves.

❧ SCRIPTURE MEMORY

MATTHEW 5:23-24—*If you are in the act of worship and become aware that your actions have caused hurt, anger, resentment, or wounded feelings in another, your awareness requires initiative. Stop your acts of worship and make your best effort to restore peace and friendship by humbling yourself and accepting responsibility for the effects of your actions. Then continue your worship.* (Paraphrase by Dave Legg, *Relational Healing Workbook*)

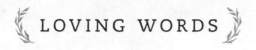 LOVING WORDS

We are meant to hold firmly to the truth in love, and to grow up in every way into Christ, the head.

EPHESIANS 4:15, *Phillips*

Out of the abundance of the heart the mouth speaketh. Out of a heart that is perfect towards God, in which the love of God is shed abroad, in which Christ dwelleth, the tongue will bring forth words of truth and uprightness, of love and gentleness, full of beauty and of blessing. God wills it. God works it. Let us claim it.

ANDREW MURRAY, *Be Perfect*

FOR ME, THE OLD SAYING "Sticks and stones may break my bones, but words will never hurt me" is not true. Unfortunately, I can still remember some hurtful words said long ago. Words said thoughtlessly and in anger can cut deep into another's soul. James described the tongue as "a small thing that makes grand speeches. But a tiny spark can set a great forest on fire" (James 3:5). If we are to love as Jesus loves, our tongue must be under control. It is out of the abundance of our heart that the mouth speaks (see Matthew 12:34, NKJV), so it is essential that love dwells abundantly in our hearts. Kind, gentle, considerate, truthful words can only spring from a heart abiding in Christ.

❧ THOUGHTFUL SPEECH

1. So often I have wished that I could retract many of the words I have spoken thoughtlessly. Look up the following Scriptures and record their insights on how to prevent hurtful words.

PROVERBS 10:19 ·· ॐ

PROVERBS 11:13 ·· ॐ

PROVERBS 15:1 ·· ॐ

PROVERBS 15:28 ·· ॐ

PROVERBS 18:13 ·· ॐ

PROVERBS 29:20 ·

---

*When you've got a word on the tip of your tongue, it's
sometimes as well to leave it there.*[1]

2. Thoughtful speech involves making some decisions about
    what is "off-limits" when conversing with others. What do
    these Scriptures teach about what we should avoid in our
    conversations?

EPHESIANS 4:31 ·

PHILIPPIANS 2:14 ·

TITUS 3:1-2 ·

--- ❧ ---

We cannot avoid forming opinions of our fellowmen, but
these should not be unjust or unkind; and, whether good
or bad, opinions need not always be expressed. It is the love
of finding fault which James here rebukes [James 4:11].[2]

CHARLES R. ERDMAN

3. The Scriptures clearly state several ways to keep from hurting others by our words. Choose two or three examples, either positive or negative, of things you have spoken recently to another person. How well did your words reflect thoughtful speech?

🌿 TRUTHFUL (BUT DIFFICULT) SPEECH

4. Speaking the truth can sometimes mean speaking words of reproof. This message is often misunderstood as condemnation and censure. There is an archaic definition of *reprove* no longer current in our usage, but I like it for

its biblical accuracy: to "convince" and "convict." This understanding carries a positive connotation of encouraging someone to get back on the right path. What does Paul's description in Ephesians 4:14-16 reveal about the purpose of speaking difficult truths?

5. Admonishing another believer takes courage, discernment, and great love. The following Scriptures give encouragement to reprove and to restore a Christian who is transgressing. Write down the guidelines and principles found in these verses concerning reproof.

PROVERBS 9:8 ....

PROVERBS 27:5-6 ....

LUKE 17:3-4 ....

6. In the verses below, there are some good reminders for the one speaking words of reproof. Write down the necessary qualities for one who speaks the truth in love.

PROVERBS 15:4 .... ✑

ROMANS 15:14 .... ✑

EPHESIANS 5:18-21 .... ✑

COLOSSIANS 3:16-17 .... ✑

The best confronters are usually people who would prefer not to have to talk to others about their sin but will do

*so out of obedience to God and love for others. . . . If you
believe that the Bible contains authoritative instruction
from God, and if you have a genuine love for God and
for your brother, you will not shirk your responsibility to
confront that brother in appropriate ways to help keep his
life in line with God's standards.[3]* KEN SANDE

7. Truth and love must go hand in hand. What can you do
   differently to ensure that your speech is thoughtful and
   truthful, for the purpose of building others up in love?

THOUGHTS AND REFLECTIONS FROM AN OLDER WOMAN

It has been a practice of mine over the years to meditate on one
verse of Scripture for an entire year. I choose each verse because
of a specific need in my life—an area that requires conforming to
the image of Christ. As I look back over the verses I have prayed
over, I realize that about every other year the verse is always on
the tongue! James said it well: "Blessing and cursing come pouring
out of the same mouth. Surely, my brothers and sisters, this is not
right!" (James 3:10). How can I be somewhat kind in one moment
and unkind in the next?

The proverb that has helped me the most in this area is Proverbs
15:28: "The heart of the godly thinks carefully before speaking;
the mouth of the wicked overflows with evil words." If I could

only learn to think before I speak, then perhaps I would at least avoid spouting out unloving words.

One time my husband, Jack, and I were talking about some needed remodeling in our home. He commented that he wished he were as gifted as his brother-in-law when it came to being a handy-man around the house. I was getting ready to say flippantly and teasingly, "Well, maybe my next husband will be talented in that area!" But, thanks be to God, I *thought* before I spoke. Instead my reply to him was, "Honey, I love you because you build into the lives of men." I share this incident because it is one of the few I can recall where I really did think before I spoke. Thinking about speaking truly works!

My verse for this year? James 3:17 (NKJV). Part of it encourages me to be "peaceable, gentle . . . full of mercy"—good words for speaking the truth in love.

> If I can enjoy a joke at the expense of another; if I can
> in any way slight another in conversation, or even in
> thought, then I know nothing of Calvary love.[4]
>
> AMY CARMICHAEL

❧ LOVE IMPARTED

8. As you review this chapter, ask the Lord what He wants you to learn about speaking the truth in love. Is there a verse on which you need to meditate or a teaching about which you need to pray so that His love can begin to dwell in your heart in a more powerful way? Write down your thoughts and pray for God's love to invade your heart and teach you about what you personally need to become a woman who loves.

SCRIPTURE MEMORY

EPHESIANS 4:15 — *We are meant to hold firmly to the truth in love, and to grow up in every way into Christ, the head.* *(Phillips)*

CHAPTER 11

LOVE NEVER FAILS

Love never fails.

1 CORINTHIANS 13:8, NKJV

There is nothing so aggressive in the moral world as love. Man can stand
before anything sooner than love. As a sustaining, resisting, aggressive
power, love will "never fail."

DAVID THOMAS, IN *The Pulpit Commentary*

THERE'S A LITTLE SAYING THAT'S often heard these days to
sum up a subject with the brief but sweeping commentary, "It's
all about . . ."—for example, "It's all about me," or "It's all about
money," or "It's all about winning." It seems appropriate to say as
we conclude this study, "It's all about love." This is true because
essentially all the commandments ask us to love. We've studied
the supremacy and the heart of love, and we have learned that
no matter what we do, if it is not done with love, our actions are
unprofitable from an eternal perspective. God, who is love, wants
His children to love one another so that those in the world can
see and experience firsthand the love that God has shed abroad
in our hearts. Love is to reign supreme in the church and to be

79

extended to all we meet. "It's all about love," first and last: because love never fails.

THE TESTIMONY OF LOVE

1. One of the purposes of the new commandment is that love among Christians would be evident to the world around them. What do these verses teach about the kind of impact we should have on the world?

    MATTHEW 5:16 ....

    JOHN 17:20-21 ....

    2 CORINTHIANS 5:18-19 ....

    TITUS 3:8 ....

2. Jesus prayed that the church would be united in love because only through love can believers build up one another and maintain harmony. What do the following passages tell us about those who cause discord within the body?

PROVERBS 6:16-19 ·································· ∂

ROMANS 16:17-19 ································· ∂

1 TIMOTHY 1:3-7 ································· ∂

———————— ᘓᏰᎧ ————————

Let the Church be true to its high calling; so shall the glory of the indwelling Christ shine through it upon the dark world, drawing all men to him. Upon every section of the Church, and every individual member of the body, according to its measure, this responsibility rests.[1]   J. WAITE

3. Many years ago I remember singing the song, "They'll Know We Are Christians by Our Love." What are some ways in which the world can see that we love one another, and by that love be drawn to the gospel?

✹ THE POWER OF LOVE

4. God's love has the power to keep us close to Him for eternity and close to one another in the body of Christ on earth. What do the following verses reveal about the blessings of abiding in God's love?

ZEPHANIAH 3:17 .... ⟳

ROMANS 15:5-7 .... ⟳

1 PETER 1:3-9 .... ⟳

5. The command to love as Jesus loves calls for consecration and perseverance. As you read through the comforting truths in Romans 8:35-39, describe the powerful nature of God's unfailing love.

6. Overwhelming victory is ours through Christ, who loves us. Review your study of the Scriptures and describe the key biblical truths that give you confidence as you seek to become a woman who loves.

Even as the whole Christian life, so love has its two stages. There is love seeking, struggling, and doing its best to obey, and ever failing. And there is love finding, resting, rejoicing, and ever triumphing. This takes place when self and its efforts have been given into the grave of Jesus, and His life and love have taken their place. The birth of heavenly love in the soul has come. In the power of the heavenly life, to love is natural and easy. Christ dwells in the heart; now we are rooted and grounded in love, and know the love that passeth knowledge.[2]

ANDREW MURRAY

THOUGHTS AND REFLECTIONS
FROM AN OLDER WOMAN

A friend told me about a young Christian wife and mother of young children who had to have major surgery. Although her husband was not a Christian, she attended a small church. When she had the operation, the women of the church began to bring meals and help out with the children. The meals and ministry did not stop after she returned home, and they continued as she was recuperating.

After a few weeks of this steady support, the husband was overcome by the love and concern that he and his family were receiving. He came to church, and he came to the Savior. He could not resist the power of love.

Love is the fabric that enfolds the body and provides warmth and comfort. This blanket of love protects against the coldness of the world and insulates from the blustery winds of hate. Its fabric is soft yet strong, and there is great beauty in its many colors and intricate patterns. It is meant to be shared, for in the sharing it covers sin and envelops all who want to know the blessings that it alone can give.

This covering of love is large enough to include all who desire its consolation yet small enough to accommodate each one personally and abundantly. To be enfolded in this blanket is to experience acceptance and healing. It neither binds nor constricts and amazingly permits those encompassed within its folds to move in freedom.

This blanket of love cannot be bought, but it is freely bestowed by the heavenly Weaver and its durability has stood the test of the ages. It is the one and only blanket that is needed for life. Without it the soul will grow cold and hard, and all that is accomplished will ultimately profit nothing. With it the soul will experience the intensity and tenderness of God's love and will ultimately be filled with the fullness of God. This love is the greatest of all virtues: it is transforming; it is powerful; and it never fails.

> If we do not show love to one another, the world has a right to question whether Christianity is true.[3]
>
> FRANCIS SCHAEFFER

 LOVE IMPARTED

7. As you review this chapter, ask the Lord what He wants you to learn concerning the unfailing nature of love. Is there a verse on which you need to meditate or a teaching about which you need to pray so that His love can begin to dwell in your heart in a more powerful way? Write down your thoughts and pray for God's love to invade your heart and teach you about what you personally need to become a woman who loves.

SCRIPTURE MEMORY

1 CORINTHIANS 13:8—*Love never fails. (NKJV)*

The Child spoke:

Father, my heart is not the same.

Good, My child; please tell Me what you have learned.

First, I realize how essential it is to Your Kingdom that I love as
You love. I understand that it grieves You when I do not
love. I am now aware that it hinders Your body when I do
not love.

Yes, My heart longs for My children to extend My love to others.

I have also learned that the only way I can receive the love that
blesses is by abiding in the Vine. And the only way to
produce the fruit of love is by being a faithful branch.

And how has your heart changed?

I no longer desire to live in order to *get* love. Now I want to *give*
love—*Your* love, that takes no thought for myself. Your love
that heals, unifies, and transforms. I want to love as *You*
love.

*My child, how it pleases Me to hear your words. Be assured that
nothing will ever separate you from My love. Keep yourself in
My love and you will fulfill My command to love one another
as I have loved you.*

About the Author

CYNTHIA HALL HEALD is a native Texan. She and her husband, Jack, a veterinarian by profession, are on staff with The Navigators in Tucson, Arizona. They have four children—Melinda, Daryl, Shelly, and Michael—as well as eleven grandchildren.

Cynthia graduated from the University of Texas with a BA in English. She frequently speaks at church women's seminars and conferences, both nationally and internationally.

She loves to be with her family, share the Word of God, have tea parties, and eat out.

BIBLE STUDIES, BOOKS, VIDEOS, AND AUDIOS

by Cynthia Heald

BIBLE STUDIES:
Becoming a Woman of Excellence
Becoming a Woman of Faith
Becoming a Woman of Freedom
Becoming a Woman of Grace
Becoming a Woman of Prayer
Becoming a Woman of Purpose
Becoming a Woman of Simplicity
Becoming a Woman of Strength
Becoming a Woman Who Loves
Becoming a Woman Whose God Is Enough
Intimacy with God
Walking Together (adapted from *Loving Your Husband* and *Loving Your Wife* by Jack and Cynthia Heald)

BOOKS AND DEVOTIONALS:
Becoming a Woman Who Walks with God (a gold-medallion-winning devotional)
Drawing Near to the Heart of God
Dwelling in His Presence
I Have Loved You
Maybe God Is Right After All
Promises to God
Uncommon Beauty

VIDEO DOWNLOADS AND DVDs OF THE FOLLOWING STUDY ARE
AVAILABLE AT CYNTHIAHEALD.COM:
Becoming a Woman Whose God Is Enough

VIDEO DVDs OF THE FOLLOWING STUDIES ARE AVAILABLE FROM
NAVPRESS:
Becoming a Woman of Simplicity
Becoming a Woman of Strength

AUDIO DOWNLOADS OF THE FOLLOWING STUDIES ARE AVAILABLE
AT CYNTHIAHEALD.COM:
Becoming a Woman of Simplicity
Becoming a Woman of Strength
Becoming a Woman Whose God Is Enough

Notes

CHAPTER 1—THE SUPREMACY OF LOVE

1. Mike Mason, *The Mystery of Marriage* (Portland, OR: Multnomah, 1985), 61–62.
2. Earl D. Radmacher, Ronald B. Allen, and H. Wayne House, eds., *The Nelson Study Bible: New King James Version* (Nashville: Thomas Nelson, 1997), 127.
3. C. S. Lewis, *The Four Loves* (San Diego: Harcourt, 1988), 127.
4. Henry Drummond, *The Greatest Thing in the World* (Grand Rapids, MI: Revell, 2000), 29.

CHAPTER 2—A NEW COMMANDMENT

1. William M. Fletcher, *The Second Greatest Commandment* (Colorado Springs: NavPress, 1983), 49.
2. Oswald Chambers, *My Utmost for His Highest* (Westwood, NJ: Barbour & Co., 1935), September 20.
3. Paul E. Miller, *Love Walked Among Us* (Colorado Springs: NavPress, 2001), 34.

CHAPTER 3—THE SOURCE OF LOVE

1. Dietrich Bonhoeffer, *Life Together* (New York: Harper & Row, 1954), 23–24.
2. C. Clemance, in *The Pulpit Commentary*, ed. H. D. M. Spence and Joseph S. Exell (Peabody, MA: Hendrickson, n.d.), 22:110.
3. Charles Wesley, "And Can It Be That I Should Gain?" in *Hymns for the Family of God* (Nashville: Paragon Associates, 1976), 260.
4. A. W. Tozer, *The Knowledge of the Holy* (New York: Harper & Row, 1961), 105.

CHAPTER 4—BEARING FRUIT

1. R. Finlayson, in *The Pulpit Commentary*, ed. H. D. M. Spence and Joseph S. Exell (Peabody, MA: Hendrickson, n.d.), 20:285.

2. Albert Barnes, *Notes on the New Testament* (Grand Rapids, MI: Baker, 1998), 10:140.
3. Bruce Wilkinson, *Secrets of the Vine* (Sisters, OR: Multnomah, 2001), 21.

CHAPTER 5—THE CHARACTER OF LOVE

1. Earl D. Radmacher, Ronald B. Allen, and H. Wayne House, eds.,*The Nelson Study Bible: New King James Version* (Nashville: Thomas Nelson, 1997), n.p.
2. Albert Barnes, *Notes on the New Testament* (Grand Rapids, MI: Baker, 1998), 11:254.
3. Henry Drummond, *The Greatest Thing in the World* (Grand Rapids, MI: Revell, 2000), 56–57.

CHAPTER 6—LOVING THE SAINTS

1. H. Bremner, in *The Pulpit Commentary*, ed. H. D. M. Spence and Joseph S. Exell (Peabody, MA: Hendrickson, n.d.), 19:413.
2. John J. Hugo, in *Quotes for the Journey; Wisdom for the Way*, compiled by Gordon S. Jackson (Colorado Springs: NavPress, 2000), 105.
3. Oswald Chambers, *My Utmost for His Highest* (Westwood, NJ: Barbour & Co., 1935), July 23.

CHAPTER 7—LOVE IN ACTION

1. Mike Mason, *The Mystery of Marriage* (Portland, OR: Multnomah, 1985), 63.

CHAPTER 8—LOVE FORGIVES

1. Ken Sande, *The Peacemaker* (Grand Rapids, MI: Baker, 1991), 186–87.
2. Lawrence O. Richards, *Expository Dictionary of Bible Words* (Grand Rapids, MI: Zondervan, 1985), 291.
3. Floyd McClung, *Learning to Love People You Don't Like* (Seattle: YWAM Publishing, 1992), 55–56.

CHAPTER 9—LOVE RECONCILES

1. Walter Hilton, *Toward a Perfect Love* (Portland, OR: Multnomah, 1985), 150.
2. A. Lukyn Williams, in *The Pulpit Commentary*, ed. H. D. M. Spence and Joseph S. Exell (Peabody, MA: Hendrickson, n.d.), 15:281.
3. Ken Sande, *The Peacemaker* (Grand Rapids, MI: Baker, 1991), 144.
4. Dietrich Bonhoeffer, *Life Together* (New York: Harper & Row, 1954), 36.
5. Charles H. Brent, in *Joy and Strength*, ed. Mary Wilder Tileston (Minneapolis: World Wide Publications, 1929), 351.

CHAPTER 10—LOVING WORDS

1. Anonymous, in *Quotable Quotations*, compiled by Lloyd Cory (Wheaton, IL: Victor, 1990), 404.

2. Charles R. Erdman, *The General Epistles: An Exposition* (Philadelphia: The Westminster Press, 1966), 48.
3. Ken Sande, *The Peacemaker* (Grand Rapids, MI: Baker, 1991), 138–39.
4. Amy Carmichael, *If* (Grand Rapids, MI: Zondervan, 1972), n.p.

CHAPTER 11—LOVE NEVER FAILS
1. J. Waite, in *The Pulpit Commentary*, ed. H. D. M. Spence and Joseph S. Exell (Peabody, MA: Hendrickson, n.d.), 19:415.
2. Andrew Murray, *Be Perfect* (Minneapolis: Bethany Fellowship, 1965), 143.
3. Francis Schaeffer, in *Quotes for the Journey; Wisdom for the Way*, compiled by Gordon S. Jackson (Colorado Springs: NavPress, 2000), 106.

Become the Woman God Created You to Be

A goal worth pursuing. Society beckons us to succeed—to achieve excellence in our appearance, our earning power, our family life. God Himself also beckons us to be women of excellence. But what exactly is He asking? If you're hungry for God's perspective on success, dig into God's Word with bestselling Bible teacher Cynthia Heald and experience the joy of becoming a woman of excellence.